Animal Babies

Claire Craig

BARNES
&NOBLE
BOOKS

NEW YORK

This 2005 edition published by
Barnes & Noble Publishing, Inc.,
by arrangement with Fog City Press.

Barnes & Noble Publishing, Inc.
122 Fifth Avenue
New York, NY 10011

ISBN 0-7607-6717-3

Printed and bound by SNP Leefung in China

05 06 07 08 09 MCH 10 9 8 7 6 5 4 3 2 1

Contents

◀ Between November and January, the female polar bear gives birth and nurses her cubs in the den. The cubs are about ten inches long and weigh less than two pounds when they are born.

Polar Bears

Polar bears roam across the frozen oceans in the Arctic. Thick, heavy fur and a layer of fat keep them warm against the chilling winds and bitter cold. Around late October or early November, pregnant females dig dens in snowdrifts where they give birth to their cubs. The dens are much warmer and safer than being outside. The newborn cubs are covered with fine hair and their eyes are closed. They stay in the den with their mother for three months.

Polar bears blend

▼A female polar bear takes care of her cubs for more than two years. She keeps them safe from predators and teaches them how to hunt.

Polar bears are the largest meat eaters living on land.

n with the icy-white snow

Lion Cubs

Newborn lion cubs are small with spotty fur. Their eyes stay closed for a few days and they hide in grass. Like all mammals, lion cubs drink their mother's milk. They are born into a group of lions called a pride. This is made up of females and their cubs, and several males. All the females in a pride are related to each other. They feed, raise, and care for each other's cubs. Female cubs often stay with the pride, but males leave when they are three years old.

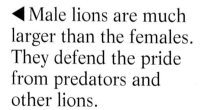

Male lions often fight with each other to win control of a pride.

◀ Male lions are much larger than the females. They defend the pride from predators and other lions.

6

▼ In the pride, lion cubs have many "mothers" instead of just one. They drink milk from the females until they are six months old.

In the Pouch

When it leaves the pouch, the young koala rides on its mother's back as she feeds on leaves.

If there is not enough food, marsupials can slow down a baby's growth in the pouch.

Mammals with pouches are called marsupials. They give birth to very tiny babies that feed on their mother's milk and grow bigger in the warm, safe pouch. A baby kangaroo, called a joey, is only one inch long when it is born. Its eyes, ears, and limbs are not fully developed, and it stays in the pouch for nine months until it is much larger and stronger. Koalas spend seven months in their mother's pouch, where they drink her milk and are safe from danger.

The pouch is a safe place

▼ Most baby kangaroos leave their mother's pouch when they are nine months old, but they stay very close to her for up to another year.

to sleep and travel

▲ The joey climbs in, front feet and head first.

▲ It twists around in the pouch.

▲ Now it is ready to jump out.

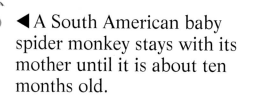

◀ A South American baby spider monkey stays with its mother until it is about ten months old.

Carrying the Young

A giant anteater gives birth standing upright, balanced by her tail.

Animal babies face great dangers. They are easy targets for predators that are bigger and stronger. Some mothers protect their young by carrying them. A newborn giant anteater crawls up onto its mother's back, where she licks it clean. The baby is the same color as its mother and seems to disappear into her fur. A spider monkey swings through the trees with her baby on her back. The baby wraps its tail around its mother, and holds on tightly.

► The baby giant anteater
stays on its mother's back
for about six months, then
gallops along beside her.
When it is two, it finds
food for itself.

11

Nesting and Hatching

Many animals lay eggs, but not all look after them. Female alligators build nests with soil and leaves, and bury their eggs near the top. They guard the nest for about 65 days and take care of their hatchlings. Sea turtles swim thousands of miles every year to return to the beach where they hatched. They scoop deep holes in the sand and lay up to 100 eggs. Then they cover the eggs with sand and return to the water. The young turtles scramble to the sea when they hatch.

Only one turtle in 100 survives long enough to become an adult.

◀ Baby cranes can run as soon as they hatch. But they do not begin to fly until they are about ten weeks old.

Only a hatchling i

▶ Birds and crabs try to
eat turtle hatchlings as
they race to the sea.

Safe in its mother's jaws

▼ A female alligator carries
her young to a quiet place,
such as a pond, where she
protects them from predators.

Apes and Monkeys

Gorillas are the largest of all the apes. They live in groups in the rainforests of Africa. Each gorilla group is led by a silverback male. He roars and slaps his chest to tell other males to keep away from his females and young. Gorilla babies are small and helpless when they are born. They stay close to their mothers. Langurs are monkeys that also live in family groups. The young are cared for by their mothers and protected by other members of the group for up to two years.

◀ Langurs give birth to one, sometimes two, babies. For the first few weeks, the baby clings tightly to its mother.

Baby gorillas ride on their mothers' backs until they are three years old.

14

▼Gorillas build nests in the trees at night to keep their babies safe from predators and away from the cold ground.

15

Living in the Sea

A female humpback can grow to be as long as a tractor-trailer. A calf is about one-third the size of its mother when it is born.

Animals that live in the sea give birth in many different places. Humpback whales swim to warm coastal waters to give birth to their calves. The mothers quickly nudge their newborn calves to the surface of the water because they need to breathe through the blowholes on the top of their heads. Although seals spend most of their time in the water, they travel to breeding grounds on land to have their pups. Seal pups can move on land and in water as soon as they are born.

◀ Northern fur seals nurse their pups on land. The pups drink their mother's rich milk and grow very quickly.

A mother seal
can tell which pup
is hers by its cry
and smell.

Baby Bears

Bears are some of the largest animals on land. But when they are born, they are blind, helpless, and tiny. A giant panda cub is the size of a mouse. A brown bear cub is as big as a guinea pig. Giant pandas give birth to one or two cubs in a sheltered place such as a cave or a hollow tree trunk. Brown bear cubs are born while their mother is sleeping through the winter. The cubs drink their mother's milk until she awakes in the spring.

▶ Giant pandas eat huge amounts of bamboo. Baby giant pandas have to chew the leaves until their teeth are strong enough to eat the stem.

18

*There are
only between 500
and 1,000 giant
pandas in the
world today.*

▲ Brown bears usually have
two cubs. The mother
teaches them how to find
food such as roots and
berries, and they stay with
her for up to four years.

Going Underground

Some animals live underground in burrows. Rabbits scamper into their burrows, called warrens, whenever they are in danger. Female European rabbits line special parts of the tunnels with grass and fur, and have their babies in these warm, soft areas. Prairie dogs also live underground. Sometimes more than 1,000 animals share many burrows, called a town, which connect up to each other. Prairie dogs sleep, look after their young, and hide from enemies in different parts of the burrows.

▶ A prairie dog stands guard at the mouth of the burrow. It calls out if an enemy is nearby.

▲ A female European rabbit can have as many as 30 young in one year.

▼ European rabbits are born with no hair, and their eyes stay closed until they are ten days old.

Rabbits have many babies because most of them do not survive.

Lively Lizards

▲ Although she helps them out of the termite mound, a female goanna does not protect her young.

The eggs of monitor lizards are sometimes eaten by other monitors.

Lizards are scaly reptiles of all shapes, sizes, and colors. Some lay eggs, while others give birth to fully formed young. The Australian blue-tongue skink has a litter of about ten live lizards among leaves, rocks, or rotting logs. These lizards can startle enemies by sticking out their bright blue tongues. Some goannas (the Australian name for monitor lizards) lay their eggs in termite mounds. When the eggs have hatched, the mother scrapes away the hard soil to help her babies out.

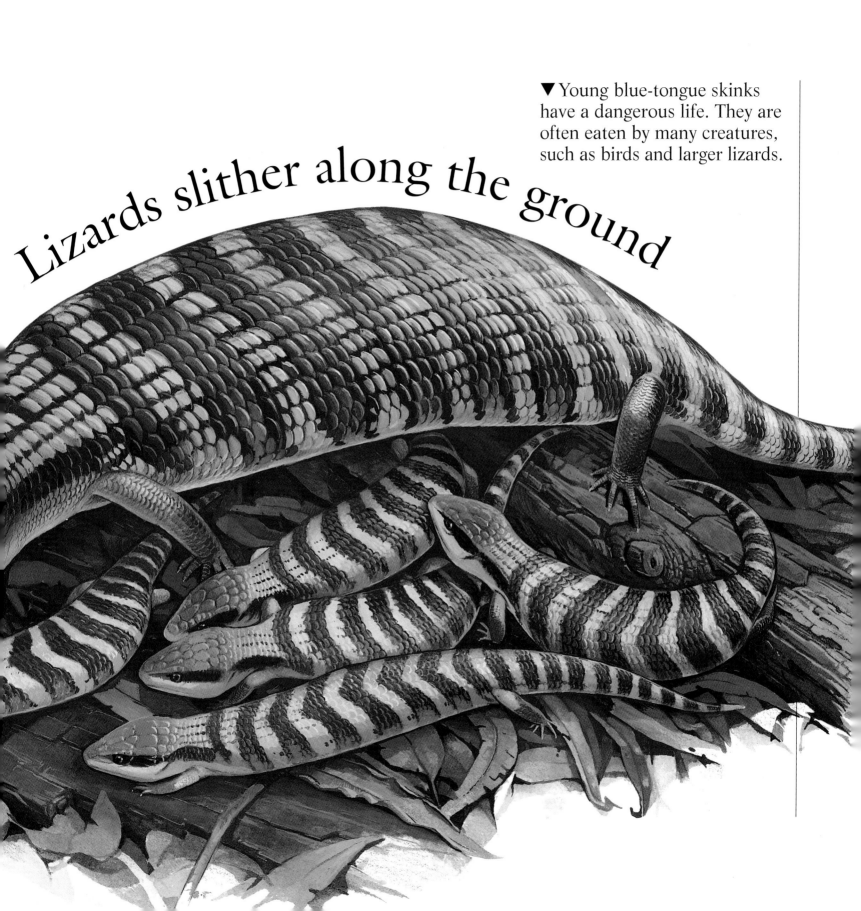

Lizards slither along the ground

▼Young blue-tongue skinks have a dangerous life. They are often eaten by many creatures, such as birds and larger lizards.

Pocketful of Fish

The fathers of some fish play an important part in looking after their young. The male arawana, a fish that lives in the flooded Amazon rainforests, sucks the female's eggs into his mouth and holds them in a special pocket he has made. The baby arawanas hatch in this pocket and stay there until they grow bigger. Female sea horses lay their eggs in a pouch on the male's belly. The babies are safe inside the pouch until it is time to leave.

◀ When baby sea horses hatch, they are pumped out through a small hole at the front of the pouch.

24

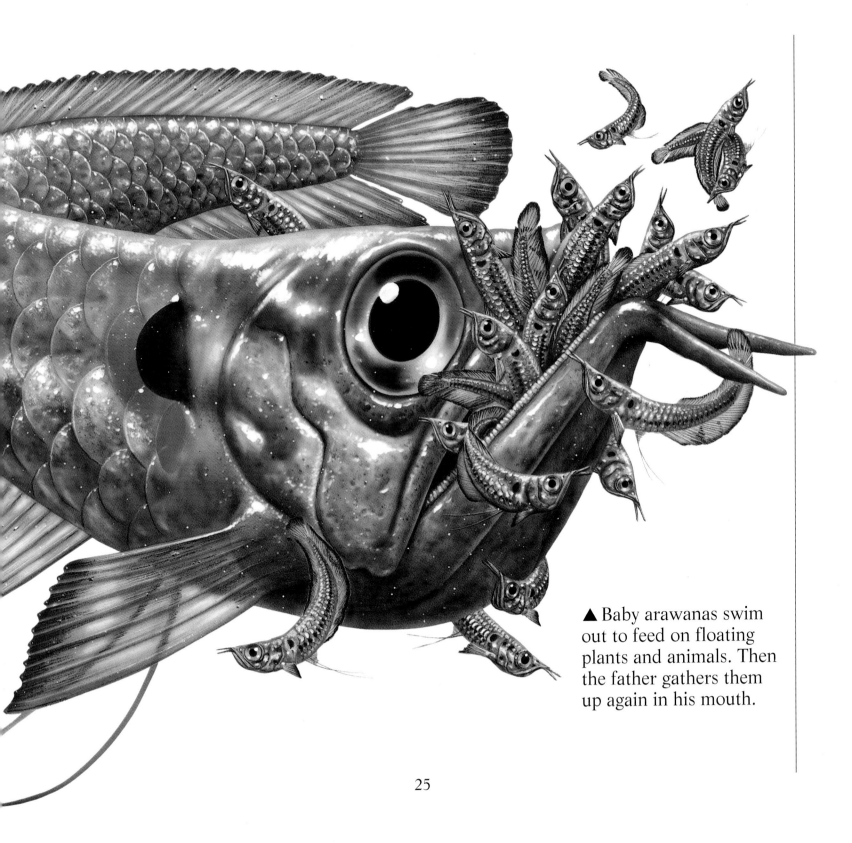

▲ Baby arawanas swim
out to feed on floating
plants and animals. Then
the father gathers them
up again in his mouth.

25

Elephants on the Move

Elephants are record holders. They are the most enormous animals on land, their pregnancies last longer than any other mammal, and they can live to be very old. Elephant calves are born into a close family of related female elephants and their children. The head of the family is the oldest female. Newborn calves are nearly blind and are looked after by their mothers and the other females in the family. They touch and smell with their trunks to learn about the world around them.

▼ Female elephants are pregnant for 22 months and usually have one calf. Like all calves, this baby bush African elephant drinks about three gallons of milk a day. It has a lot of growing to do.

▲ The Sumatran Asian elephant is one of the smallest elephants. A newborn calf has hair on its head and back.

African elephants flap their very large ears to keep cool.

Snakes Alive!

▼ Garter snakes are some of the most common snakes. They give birth to live young.

Snakes are long, legless reptiles. Some of them lay their eggs in warm places such as rotting logs, or under rocks. Others give birth to live young. Pythons wrap themselves tightly around prey to kill it, but they also wrap themselves gently around their eggs until they hatch. They are the only snakes that help the young inside the eggs to develop by keeping them warm. Like most other reptiles, snakes do not care for their young once they are born.

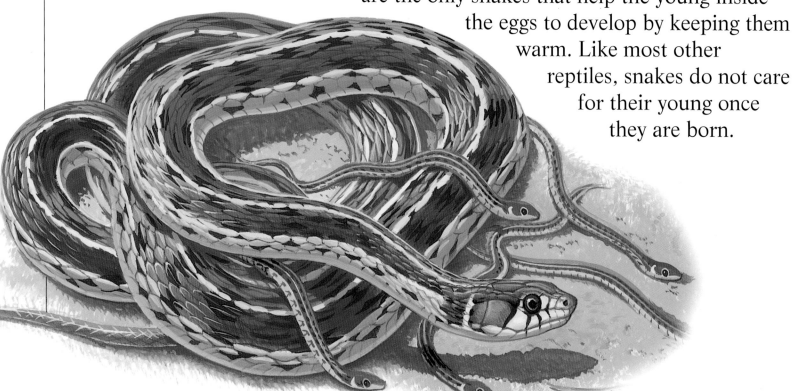

▶ Pythons coil around their eggs to keep them warm and protect them from predators. But they do not look after their young once they have hatched.

Warming the eggs with its body heat

Most snakes shed their skin soon after they are born.

◄ Young wolves join the pack to hunt large prey, such as caribou, when they are about six months old. Wolves howl together after hunting.

Family Matters

Meerkats warm

Many animals live together. In groups, they can defend themselves, care for their young, and hunt for food better than on their own. Meerkats live in burrows in southern Africa. Their newborn babies are blind and hairless and do not venture above ground until they are one month old. When meerkats leave their burrows, they stand up straight to keep a lookout for danger. Wolves also care for their young together, in groups called packs. They whimper, growl, and bark to communicate with each other.

The howls of a wolf pack can be heard for six miles.

▼ If a meerkat sees an enemy, such as a hawk or an eagle, it makes a shrill cry. The others run quickly into their burrows.

themselves in the morning sun

Other titles in the series:

INCREDIBLE CREATURES
MIGHTY DINOSAURS
SCALES AND TAILS
THINGS WITH WINGS
UNDERWATER ANIMALS

Illustrators

(t=top, b=bottom, l=left, r=right, c=center, F=front cover, B=back cover)

Martin Camm, 1, 14bl. Simone End, 2, 8tl, 9r, 13tr, 16bl, 20bc, 20/21c. Christer Eriksson, 3bl, 6bl, 6/7c, 10tl, 24bl, 25c. David Kirshner, Fb, 4/5b, 12/13c, 18/19c. Frank Knight, B, 4tl, 26/27c, 27tr, 28bl, 29tr, 30tl, 32. John Mac/Folio, 8/9c, 11c, 19tr. Barbara Rodanska, 12bl. Trevor Ruth, 30/31b. Peter Schouten, 3tr, 14/15c, 22tl, 22/23c. Rod Scott, 16/17c. Guy Troughton, F.